MOON IN SCORPIO

RHEA DELÉO

Copyright © 2019 Rhea Deléo. Printed in the United States of America. All rights reserved. No part of this publication may be reproduced, redistributed, or transmitted in any form or by any means, including photocopying, recording, or other electronic or mechanical methods, without the prior written permission of the author, except in the case of excerpts embodied in critical reviews, research, other academic or scholarly purposes, and certain other noncommercial uses permitted by copyright law.

MOON IN SCORPIO

dedicated to the loveless

CONTENTS

me 11

him 38

her 69

dear reader,

"moon in scorpio" is a collection of poems and my original song lyrics focusing on the darker complexities of love. this book touches on themes such as self-image issues, sexuality, unrequited love, growth, and forgiveness. it is a personal look at the thoughts, emotional experiences, and calamities i had growing up, that inspired me to begin writing in the first place.

being an avid lover of astrology from a young age, i used to blame my struggle to understand myself on my moon being in scorpio, one of the most mysterious and misunderstood signs in the zodiac. moon signs in a horoscope represent your inner world, the hidden part of you most people don't see. having moon in scorpio, i have always had the desire to understand my own and others feelings. the best way i have been able to channel these energies is through my art, and music and writing have allowed me to embrace my feelings without trying hide or mask them.

this book tells part of my story as i am still learning about love and myself. this collection is divided into three sections for the three biggest stages of my life so far, that i feel will resonate with anyone. the first chapter "me." represents my past insecurities as a growing woman who was struggling to discover and appreciate herself. in the second chapter, the man that represents "him." is not one singular person, but rather several unattainable individuals i gave my heart to. the poems in this chapter capture the raw feelings i experienced inside my relationships with them. the final chapter "her." is based on the thoughts that have now as a woman who is learning to grow from the heartbreaks of her past to become a stronger, happier person.

i hope that you will read this book with an open mind and heart, and that my poems will resonate with you in some way. the words that you are about to read come from the deepest part of me. even now, it both excites and scares me a little to open up like this. whether it's through my poetry, music, or just daily conversations though, i want people to know that it is okay to express your vulnerability and pain. that you can use your feelings to connect with the world on deeper, more compassionate level.

with much love,

rhea

"and now you are and i am,
and we are a mystery
that will never happen
again."
- e. e. cummings

MOON IN SCORPIO

me.

sometimes
the duality
of my nature
feels anything but

n a t u r a l

i used to gaze at photos of
my mother from when she
was my age

i would wonder why i didn't

have her modelesque frame

unblemished face

and glowing maturity for
someone so young

would i ever become
that beautiful?

i could
conquer the world

if i could only
conquer
the civil war
inside of myself

MOON IN SCORPIO

i've been alone
for much too long
nothing like
d e p r i v a t i o n
to inspire
sad songs

i'm not
f r a g i l e
but please

handle me
    with care

i step
on the scale
again
as if there would be
much of a difference
from when
i stepped
on the scale
yesterday

why do i
let a number
bring me so much

d i s a p p o i n t m e n t ?

RHEA DELÉO

i feel as stable
as an earthquake

it's a shame
the moments
when we look
the most
b e a u t i f u l
often happen when
we can't see them

imagine if we could

don't try to erase it
the smile on your face is
a mask of how you
really feel

come out and
just say it
there's no need
to fake it
if it's real

MOON IN SCORPIO

i don't have
a one-track mind
it's more like

a cyclone

how can someone
so happy do
s a d n e s s
so very well

MOON IN SCORPIO

is it so hard
to believe
that a woman
can change the color
of her hair or cut

it   all   off

without it
having anything
to do with
a man?

darling
you give your
trust away
too easily

MOON IN SCORPIO

leos are

confident
extraverted
always optimistic

d a m n

i can't even
relate to my own
zodiac sign

perhaps depression
would be less
of a problem
if parents
told their children

i'm here for you

instead of

s u c k it u p

MOON IN SCORPIO

why are
some of the
l o v e l i e s t people
you'll ever meet

also the
l o n e l i e s t

no amount
of tissue can fix
your body issues

true sexiness
should have
more to do
with your attitude
than with the
revealing things
you put on
your body

RHEA DELÉO

for the longest time
i thought i hated
being touched

that was when
i actually needed
touch the most

i feel
the rocky terrain
of my face
when i wake up

my hands wearily travel
over the scarlet bumps and
valleys pitted in my skin

i'm 23 years old
when will this end

i honestly
miss my innocence

a girl with
peachy creamy skin
once told me
i shouldn't cover
my face with
so much m a k e - u p

honey
you really wouldn't
understand
why i do

aphrodite
has thick thighs
so why the hell
can't i

i wrote

i l o v e y o u
on my bathroom mirror
in red lipstick
this morning

maybe now
i'll look at myself
and start to believe
that i do

i'm the queen
of not knowing
what i want

my hips
are t o o b i g
and my chest
t o o s m a l l

yet i underestimated
how much men
love to devour
pears

RHEA DELÉO

him.

he saw me shining
through the dark
when no one else could
i had never felt so desired

MOON IN SCORPIO

i remember
the first time
i tried to kiss you
in public

you quickly
turned away

you didn't want
your friends to see

it was below zero
outside and i was
f r e e z i n g c o l d

i wore less so i
would look good
for him

it wasn't worth it

he said
does it scare you
that i can break
your heart
like fine china

a m i l l i o n p i e c e s

are you afraid
of the way you'll
shatter if i
throw you down?

RHEA DELÉO

the way he'd tear
my clothes off
and toss them
across the floor
was his favorite
form of
a r t

the mastery
with which
he navigated
my mind and body
was so rehearsed

it was clear
he'd been playing
the role for years

and i was
a captive audience

yet i wondered
how many other girls
had come to his show

sometimes
while you slept
next to me
i would stare up
at the ceiling
of your bedroom
silently
asking myself

what am i doing here

when will it be
my turn
to be cared for
to be

s a t i s f i e d

why won't
you even try

it shouldn't be so hard
for this man to say
that he loves me

you can't fix
c o m p l i c a t i o n
without
c o m m u n i c a t i o n

when your lips
meet mine
there's nothing
behind it

am i just a way
to pass the time
until you find

the next
love of your life?

MOON IN SCORPIO

the sad part
is that i know
exactly what he's
doing with that girl
she'll be his next

miss take

it was dawn
and you were
in the shower
i was laying
on your bed
i opened my eyes
to see someone else's
strands of
long blond hair
mingling with yours
on the pillowcase
i plucked one up

and broke it in two

he got
the best of me

why'd i
have to get
the worst of him

your eyes were closed but
they opened up to see me
looking down at you
frozen bliss
you were happy
to feel me near

could it be
that way again?
or is that supposed
to change
when you become

j u s t f r i e n d s

MOON IN SCORPIO

as soon as it didn't feel like
making love anymore
i was done

i wasn't the first
to hold him

i guess i'm not
going to be
the last

my mother
always warned me
not to mess with
dangerous things
how was i
supposed to know

that you would be
one of them

i watched
as the last
ember of hope
i had for us
died out
in front of me

our story in ashes

minute men
there's a timer
on their hearts
love like clockwork
here and then
it's gone

you can't count on
minute men

now that you're gone
this house feels
so damn cold

do you realise
you took the
warmth with you?

MOON IN SCORPIO

i'm clinging
to the past
like the smell
of your cologne
still clings to me
it's beginning to fade

just like our memories

just like your face

RHEA DELÉO

i once stayed up
all night casting spells
trying to forget
about it all

sometimes
i say too much

but i'd be lying
if i said
i don't still love you

i can't throw anything out
because i have nothing
to remember you by
it's almost like
you were never here

but like the wind
even though you
can't see it
you can still feel it
and how it

touched
        your
                skin

i wish i could
delete my feelings
as quickly as i
delete the words
i type when i'm
missing you

he used to be my
every hope and dream
it's funny how some things
never become reality

i had finally
sewn up
the torn patches
of my
body and soul

yet here
he was again
eager to
rip the stitches

when i'm sober

i'll say i don't
give a damn
about him

when i'm drunk

i'll tell you
the truth

as much as i wanted to
hate him for the pain
he'd caused me

the angel
on my shoulder
whispered

he's a hurt soul
just like you
dear

RHEA DELÉO

her.

persistence
isn't always key
sometimes
what you want
is actually
toxic for you

you're not
going to find
the antidote
for his poison

in the lips
of another man

friend or lover
you can't
fill the void
they leave by
trying to fill it

with someone else

i have a
perfectly good bed

but i have too
many memories
with him in it

sometimes healing
means sleeping
on the couch
until you start

f o r g e t t i n g

you will never
find the comfort
you desperately need
in the arms
of the ones
who hurt you

RHEA DELÉO

i am more
than just a list
of pros and cons in
a man's book

if you want
to run away

better buy
two tickets

because you'll
be taking your
troubles with you

loving yourself
doesn't mean
you don't need
anyone

it means you
can be at peace
filling your own cup

even when others
aren't around
to help

MOON IN SCORPIO

it's easy to
disguise your
fear of growing
close to people
by calling it

i n d e p e n d e n c e

show the world
how you wish
to be cared for
by first caring
for yourself
that way

MOON IN SCORPIO

there's no use
in waiting for
someone to break you
from the chains
of your past

you have to
s a v e y o u r s e l f

it's ironic
the people we
dislike the most
we tend to be
the most like

MOON IN SCORPIO

i've had
my share of pain

now i'm going
to focus on
what i gained from it

RHEA DELÉO

the real triumph
is learning
how to balance
the happiness
of others
with your own

MOON IN SCORPIO

to those
who try to
make you believe
that you are
hard to love

kindly escort
them and their
n o n s e n s e
out of your life

sometimes
just your presence
is the greatest gift
you can give to
someone who is
deeply hurting

i'm finally beginning
to realise that
i'm strong enough to be
my own hero

i am
starting to give
less of myself
to those who
only want to take

MOON IN SCORPIO

i don't need some
crazy display of love
just take the time

to listen to me

you are a goddess
you have the power
to make men

worship you

without them ever

entering your temple

i am becoming
a great lover

of life

of others

of myself

many artists
find their inspiration
in the sunlight

i found mine
through exploring
the darkness

MOON IN SCORPIO

i don't think
i will ever have myself
completely figured out

damn

i do love
a good mystery

it's funny how
the men of my past
never wanted
to listen to my music

now they ask
if my songs
are about them

MOON IN SCORPIO

it's been so long
but i'm starting
to feel my childhood
e x c i t m e n t
about the future again

i'm not proud
of some of my choices
but i am proud
that i am choosing
to learn from them

MOON IN SCORPIO

how can i
help the world
i asked my mother

with your words
with your music
with your art

she replied

the end.

you've taken a glimpse into my heart. into
my soul. thank you. i have poured my words
out and you have received them with a
warm embrace. with compassion. with empathy. i
hope you know how loved you are. i hope you realise
you can rise above your worst moments and
that they don't define you. don't be afraid
to share your heart with the world dear,
even if it is fragile. even if you don't trust it
anymore. there is endless beauty in
everyone, and we are all here to help each
other begin to recognise and celebrate that
beauty.

Rhea Deléo is the pen name for poet, songwriter, and recording artist Shannon Ferguson, who is passionate about bringing light to the darker emotions and complexities of human nature. "Moon in Scorpio" is her first published book, released in November, 2019.

A graduate from Converse College, she received her Bachelor's degree in Contemporary Music. When she isn't composing or writing, she is actively performing and sharing her own personal music with the world.

Instagram:
@rhea.deléo
@shannonfergusonofficial

Printed in Dunstable, United Kingdom